The Revisionist

JESSE EISENBERG

The Revisionist

A Play

Introduction by
John Patrick Shanley

Grove Press
New York

Printed in the United States of America
Published simultaneously in Canada

ISBN: 978-0-8021-2233-9
eBook ISBN: 978-0-8021-9273-8

Grove Press
an imprint of Grove/Atlantic, Inc.
154 West 14th Street
New York, NY 10011

Distributed by Publishers Group West

www.groveatlantic.com

13 14 15 16   10 9 8 7 6 5 4 3 2 1

INTRODUCTION

How to read a play? I've done it enough to tell you how I do it. I read with a degree of fatalism. It's like visiting family. Occasionally, the experience is rewarding, but always, suffering is involved. You're trapped in somebody else's house or head, their engine of despair or uplift. Face-to-face with a wise uncle, ignorant nephew or enigmatic aunt, you wonder how you fit in, or if you do. You see yourself in an uncomfortable light. You're a hapless intruder. If the play is good, at some point you realize you're in it. Shit. This is MY house.

Buckyballs began bouncing in my head scarcely moments into the production of *The Revisionist* I saw some weeks back. A character named David, a young man who is utterly unable to be present, gets trapped in a very small space with an old woman named Maria, who is ONLY present. As in all the best stuff, the encounter is rich because each character highlights the other.

David is a product of life in America now, a new kind of Peter Pan who flies because he can't land. He can't grow up because he can't commit to any one life long enough to do so. His entire method of operation consists of running, deflecting and avoiding, by every means possible. In a bold stroke, Jesse Eisenberg not only wrote the play, but played the part. His performance physically demonstrated the emotional truth of this guy; he literally spent a goodly amount of his time onstage finding a way, again in a very small space, of staying off the floor. He was habitually PERCHING on something: a bed, the arm of a chair or couch. When that tactic proved impossible, he resorted to tranquilizing himself with marijuana or liquor.

Meanwhile, his counterpart, Maria, a Polish woman in her seventies, wants the one thing the young man can't give. She wants company. She wants to get to know him, to be with him, to share food and time with him. Her values are all human.

She's thrilled because this young fellow is her cousin, and he has elected to visit her. She has been suffering from isolation and longs to connect. Her plight is such because she lost her European family in the Holocaust. David is her American family. But Maria wants family in the European sense, and David can't begin to fulfill that need.

Now, the institution of family in America has been under assault for a long time, but these days there is an additional malaise. Individuals are now losing their connection to humanness itself. The extraordinary onslaught of virtual communication and social media has allowed us to cultivate something unhealthy in our psyches: the desire NOT to be touched. Not only does David express a lack of care or interest in his own family, his alienation goes well beyond that to a loss of connection with the entire human race. He is a true narcissist. He is utterly alone, trapped in a world empty of people, alone with his vague dreams of fame and fortune. Other people exist for him only as props or impediments on his way forward toward glory and comfort. He is a writer, and tellingly, his first book contained no people, only animals.

Fortunately, David's humanity has not yet been obliterated. Maria has framed a review he got for his book, and wants him to sign it. He refuses because it is a bad review. But in a private moment, he relents and signs. Compassion, weakened but not extinguished, still occasionally animates his world. This lends the piece hope. David may at last land somewhere and relate to another person in a meaningful way. The future is not yet written in ink.

It's the oldest story. Two lonely people meet. Will they provide comfort and community for each other, or will they fail? The reason this play needed to be written was not the predicament, but the obstacles standing in the way of a solution. The need is old. The obstacles to intimacy are new.

We are living in sterile times. Physically, the most recent thinking on the biological front is that our immune systems are increasingly being disarmed by insufficient exposure to bacteria. We aren't being challenged enough to exercise our defenses. To put it another way, we're losing our talent for building a relationship with the wild world. Emotionally, portable devices are providing a similar insulation from social contact. We are losing the ability to BE with other people.

The Revisionist presents a young man who has lost his way try to negotiate his time with another person, a substantial person, without emotional cost to himself. At last, this woman bares her soul to David in an effort to build a bridge. David, because of his loss of PRESENCE, is unaffected. Her reaction is to throw him out. Good for her. With luck, this will be the prompt that ultimately brings David back to his humanity.

I think whom you will identify with depends on what your problems are. If you are desperately trying to find a way to connect with others, and you are getting text messages back, you will probably be feeling Maria. If you don't understand why you should just sit with people for significant periods of time in order to get to know them, David's your guy.

Read the play. You'll be stimulated.
John Patrick Shanley

The Revisionist

Please note that the italicized lines of dialogue are spoken in Polish. An appendix of the Polish translations is included in this volume.

PRODUCTION CREDITS

The Revisionist had its world premiere at the Cherry Lane Theatre, presented by Rattlestick Playwrights, opening on February 28, 2013. The production was directed by Kip Fagan; sets by John McDermott; costumes by Jessica Pabst; lighting by Matt Frey; sound by Bart Fasbender; stage manager, Christine Catti; production manager, Eugenia Furneaux.

The cast was as follows:

DAVID Jesse Eisenberg

MARIA Vanessa Redgrave

ZENON Dan Oreskes

SCENE I

A television is on, playing CNN International:

CNN Long saddled with its image as one of Asia's poorest nations, Vietnam's economy in the last decade has come along in leaps and bounds. Foreign investors' eyes are lighting up at the prospect of grabbing a piece of the action now that Vietnam has been voted into the World Trade Organization.

A loud buzzer is sounded. The television continues. The buzzer rings again. A lamp comes on, dimly lighting:

A three-room cramped apartment in Szczecin, Poland, a large, run-down city on the Baltic Sea. A living room and small bedroom flank a narrow kitchen. The kitchen table is set for two.

There are framed photographs on every surface and wall.

Maria jumps off the couch and switches on a light. She frantically moves to her apartment's intercom, pressing it—buzz. She fixes herself at a small mirror and lights a candle on the table. There is a knock at the door and she swings it open.

MARIA I never wanted to die so much!

David stands at the door, offstage.

DAVID Hello, Maria.

MARIA You had me that my heart was in my mouth!

DAVID It's nice to see you. Thank you. In advance.

MARIA I was going to stick my head in the oven, but it take so long to heat, I change my mind. You three hours late!

DAVID Yeah, sorry, my plane was delayed. I didn't have your telephone number. Can I please come inside?

MARIA I give you my phone number so you should have it.

3

Maria rushes to a small notepad in the kitchen as David enters holding a suitcase and shouldering a book bag.

He is dressed sloppily, a hoodie obscuring his face.

DAVID Well I don't need it now, I don't need it anymore. I'm here, Maria.

MARIA Still, I give you. Maybe for the emergency.

She scribbles her number and thrusts it at him.

MARIA (*cont.*) You can read this?

DAVID Sure, it's legible.

MARIA You could use in America too, you know.

DAVID That's fine.

MARIA Now you look at me.

DAVID Yeah, my bags are kind of heavy—

MARIA Stand straight up, your back. Look at me.

DAVID I have a laptop in here—

Maria gently pulls back his hoodie and holds his shoulders.

MARIA You look like him. Your grandfather. Is like a picture.

DAVID (*squirming away*) I'd like to put my bags down now.

MARIA Of course, you put in your room.

DAVID Okay, thank you.

MARIA (*leading him into the bedroom*) Did you think you would not have your own room?

DAVID I didn't consider it.

MARIA You probably think we all live in a small hut in Poland.

DAVID No, I guess I kind of thought I would have a room.

MARIA Well it's a terrible tiny room. But you put your bags down. You talk to me about something. I want to know your trip, your family, your work—

DAVID (*dryly*) It's all very exciting.

MARIA But first I shut the television off. I was watching American television. CNN.

She raises the volume on the television to impress David.

DAVID Yes, I can hear it.

MARIA (*shuts the TV off*) I must be sorry, David. My English is sometimes like cows.

DAVID Excuse me?

MARIA I speak English like a cow. Is very hard language. No one speak to me—no one speak to me Polish also—but I learn quick. They tell me knife. I read ka-nife. I don't understand, is stupid. My fault also—I don't know. Are you hungry? What you eat?

DAVID I ate a little bit on the plane.

MARIA Sha, on the plane! What you want?

DAVID Nothing, really, I'm fine. Just a little tired.

MARIA I make you dinner. I make you a special dinner. (*suddenly jubilant*) That you come to visit me, David. I am so happy you come to me!

DAVID Thank you. I'm happy I'm going to finish my book.

Maria stares at him, taken aback.

DAVID (*cont.*) What I mean is—I don't mean to be—I'm just kind of swamped at the moment and it's on my mind. Sorry. I've been overwhelmed. But I'm happy to see you too. And to be here. Maria.

MARIA (*considers him*) This is a good thing you do. To have the blood back in the house! This is good thing, David.

Maria enters the kitchen and pulls out a cooked chicken from the oven. She takes out a small bag of parsley and begins sprinkling it over the chicken.

In a mirror image, David, in his room, searches through his suitcase and pulls out a long sock. He takes a hollowed-out jar of Hellmann's mayonnaise from the sock and then removes from the jar a bag, which contains some marijuana, a little pipe and a lighter.

He sprinkles some weed in his pipe.

In the kitchen, Maria puts the chicken into the microwave, powering it on.

David, in his bedroom, tries to open the window to smoke, but the handle is too high. He climbs on the windowsill to reach the window but it is stuck shut. He rattles the handle but it won't budge as—

MARIA (*cont.*) Ah! I forget. David! David! I forget! I have present for you—

David hops off the sill just as Maria enters his room, carrying a composition notebook.

MARIA (*cont.*) To write your book.

DAVID Oh. That's very thoughtful.

MARIA I buy it from the post office. You will use it to write the book?

DAVID I don't know. I really just write on the computer.

MARIA I think the paper is maybe better.

DAVID Maybe.

MARIA And no one want to steal paper from you.

DAVID That's true. Computers can be a risky investment.

MARIA So we agree. What did you get for me?

DAVID I didn't know we were doing gifts. (*pause; she waits*) Okay. I got you—(*hesitates, pulls a bottle from his suitcase*) Some vodka. Some Polish vodka. It's very famous, I think. And very tasty, Polish vodka.

MARIA But I live in Poland.

DAVID You do.

MARIA So why you get me Polish vodka?

DAVID (*for his own amusement*) To further celebrate your heritage.

MARIA Hmm. I think this is more a present for you. But thank you.

DAVID I'm glad you like it.

MARIA I don't drink too much. Who do I drink with? Jerzy, he drink every night—not vodka always, beer, nalevka—but when he die, I stop drinking. No one should drink vodka if they are alone. Beer, is okay you drink alone, but vodka is a drink that is sad with no one. But you drink with me, David. Will be nice.

DAVID I look forward to that. So I think I'm going to change clothes, if that's all right.

MARIA Of course is all right.

She stares at him, waiting for something—

DAVID Great. I think I'll do that now.

MARIA Is a good time, I think.

Maria exits the room. David takes out his weed and pipe and jumps on the windowsill, reaching for the handle, just as Maria turns back around, reentering—

MARIA I forget I should ask you— (*seeing him on the sill*) What you doing?

DAVID Um, I was just trying to get some air. Is that not okay?

MARIA If you want, is okay. But is expensive for me. Cold air come in the flat, the heat go up, the bill go up.

DAVID Right, sorry. I didn't know what the, what your utility plan was here. (*jumps down*) What did you want to ask me?

MARIA Yes. How long you should stay here?

DAVID I actually wanted to ask you about that. You know why I'm here, right?

MARIA I know what your grandfather tell me.

DAVID What was that?

MARIA You want to write a book, I think.

DAVID Yes. Sort of. I have to revise a book.

MARIA What is this?

DAVID I have to revise my book—to change what I've already written. It's not relevant to you, but I'm not just, like, starting something, I have a career. I was actually supposed to hand it in six weeks ago—

MARIA Six weeks you stay here?

DAVID No. No. My book was due six weeks ago so I don't have that much time. That's why I came here. I needed a drastic change of scenery. I need to buckle down, focus. So I was thinking of staying here for about a week.

MARIA A week? Your grandfather tell me you maybe stay longer.

DAVID No, I think a week should be fine. I imagine that's all I need.

MARIA All you need.

DAVID Anyway, I didn't want to bother you.

MARIA Is no bother to me. I want you should stay here forever!

DAVID Well, obviously, I can't do that. I'm a bit inflexible at the moment.

MARIA So when you leave me? You need to buy ticket for plane.

DAVID (*pulls out his ticket*) I have a return ticket. It's for next Wednesday.

MARIA You give me. I put on refrigerator, we should not forget it.

DAVID I'm not going to forget.

MARIA (*reaching for it*) Still, you give me.

DAVID (*holding it away from her*) This is absurd. This is really not necessary. (*beat; he gives it to her*) But thank you.

Maria reads the ticket as she walks to the kitchen to place it under a magnet on the fridge.

MARIA You leave Wednesday at nine thirty.

DAVID Yeah, I guess so.

MARIA So you maybe take taxi at six o'clock.

DAVID Okay, sure. I don't really know.

MARIA Which mean you miss dinner on Wednesday night.

DAVID I'm sure I'll be fine. I'll probably just eat on the plane.

MARIA This is the only place you eat food. (*pointed:*) You miss dinner on Wednesday.

She enters the bedroom and lifts a framed picture of David.

MARIA (*cont.*) Do you know this person?

DAVID Where did you get that?

MARIA I look at it every day before you come here. I speak to you. I say "Good morning David." I practice my English with you. You tell me knife. You learn Polish.

DAVID How did you get it?

MARIA Your grandfather send me. He call me every Sunday. My only cousin who call me. He is very special, your grandfather.

DAVID Sure.

MARIA You are different I think.

David takes the picture from Maria.

DAVID I think I look stupid.

MARIA Sha, you are young. Bad teeth is normal for kids. And fat too, but you not.

DAVID Thank you.

MARIA And look at the eyes.

DAVID What about them?

MARIA Now look at my eyes.

DAVID Where?

MARIA In my head. Look at my eyes. Do you see?

DAVID See what?

MARIA We have same eyes.

DAVID Do we?

MARIA Yes, exact same. Is blue, but ugly kind.

DAVID Really? I always thought my eyes were a nice color.

MARIA No, they ugly like mine.

The telephone rings. Maria rushes to the kitchen, picking it up. In Polish:

MARIA (*cont.*)   *Hello? I am good, and how are you? Good good—Yes?*

David places the picture of himself back on the shelf and then turns it face down. He opens up his laptop, powering it on, as Maria continues on the telephone:

MARIA (*cont.*)   *No, I did receive it but I can't right now, thank you for calling. Goodbye.*

Maria hangs up as the microwave dings.

MARIA (*cont.*)   David, dinner is ready. You finish packing later.

DAVID   Actually, I think I'm okay, Maria.

MARIA   Good, you come in kitchen.

DAVID   No, I mean I'm actually not really that hungry.

MARIA   I make chicken for you.

DAVID   Really, I'm fine. Actually, I don't eat meat.

MARIA   Is chicken.

DAVID   Yeah, I don't eat chicken.

MARIA   Why, you sick?

DAVID   I'm a vegetarian. I don't eat flesh that was once alive.

MARIA   This is silly. I tell your parents.

DAVID   They know. It's not a bad thing.

MARIA   Is stupid thing. I not eat for two week when I was seven. Two week I not get nothing! You rich and say you don't eat the chicken.

DAVID   I'm sorry, Maria.

MARIA   So what you want? I make you carrots. And broccoli. You like Philadelphia?

DAVID Philadelphia?

She pulls a tub of Philadelphia cream cheese out of the refrigerator.

MARIA I spread Philadelphia on bread. This is no meat. Come, you eat, you do prayer.

DAVID What prayer?

MARIA Over the food. You do maybe a Jewish prayer.

DAVID You gotta be kidding me.

The telephone rings again. Maria picks it up:

MARIA *Hello? Yes? Fine thank you. And you? No, I'm sorry. Goodbye.* (*hangs up*)

DAVID Who keeps calling you?

MARIA They ask for money. They say is for blind people but I don't know about this.

DAVID You have telemarketing in Poland?

MARIA They call me always. But my friend say no money go to the blind people.

DAVID Yeah, it's probably a scam. Could you please just unplug your phone?

MARIA No, your grandfather call me. My family call me. I am here!

DAVID You said he calls you on Sunday.

MARIA Every Sunday!

DAVID So why don't you unplug your phone until Sunday? Until he calls you.

MARIA (*stares at David, beat*) Because maybe he call me Tuesday. Now what you want you should eat?

DAVID Nothing, Maria. But thank you. I think I'm just going to go to sleep.

MARIA But is good you eat first. We open my gift, my vodka.

DAVID I'd really like to just go to sleep, if that's okay.

MARIA (*pause, quietly*) Is okay.

DAVID I do appreciate you letting me stay here.

MARIA Is okay.

DAVID I'm glad.

MARIA David?

DAVID Yes, Maria?

MARIA Tomorrow, we take a tour to see Szczecin. My friend is taxi driver, Zenon, and he pick us up. Nine o'clock will be in front.

DAVID That sounds very nice, Maria but, like I mentioned, I don't think I can do that.

MARIA Nine is too soon. You right, I stupid. I think you want we leave early. But is okay. I call him right now, he come at ten. You sleep, you rest—

DAVID No, I don't think I can go out at all tomorrow. I need to work. This is the problem I was having in New York. I'm easily distracted. This is why I came here, Maria.

MARIA You don't want to see my city?

DAVID I do, I do. But not tomorrow. I need to work. I came here. I came here to work.

Pause. A slight challenge:

MARIA I think you came here to visit me.

DAVID We'll go another time. Maybe the weekend.

MARIA The weekend is better. I call Zenon.

David enters his bedroom and jumps back on the windowsill, balancing precariously. He finally pries the little window open.

13

In the kitchen, Maria takes David's plate and glass off the table and begins to eat alone. She mumbles to herself:

MARIA (*cont.*)   Yes, yes. The weekend is better.

David, on the sill, takes a long hit from his pipe and slowly exhales out the open window.

BLACKOUT—

SCENE 2

The next day, early afternoon

The radio plays an inane BBC daytime talk show as David tries to work in his bedroom.

Maria dusts her room, listening to the radio.

The telephone rings. Maria turns down the radio and answers the phone:

MARIA Hello? Yes, it's a good time. I know. I'm sorry, but thank you for calling. You too.

She hangs up, returns to her room and continues dusting, raising the volume on the radio.

DAVID Maria? (*she doesn't hear*) Maria! The radio is—

MARIA Yes, David?

DAVID If you don't mind, your radio is a little distracting!

MARIA What you say David?

DAVID I said the radio is very loud! It breaks my concentration! Can you please turn it down!?

MARIA I will not turn it down! I will turn it off!

DAVID Okay, thank you!

MARIA How is that solution?!

DAVID It's fine, thank you!

MARIA Is a good solution to our problem!

She turns off the radio. He resumes typing as she enters his bedroom.

MARIA (*cont.*) Do you know why all problems are the same? Because they have a solution. That is how we know is a problem in the first place.

DAVID All right.

MARIA And after you solve the problem, you think it was not so bad as when you first see it.

DAVID (*patronizing*) That's very wise. Thank you.

He resumes typing. She lingers—

MARIA Did you make the book?

DAVID What?

MARIA Did you write the book?

DAVID I'm revising the book, yes. It takes a long time.

MARIA You not finish it?

DAVID No, of course not.

MARIA You in the room three hours. I clean my flat two times.

DAVID Well, it takes a little more than three hours to finish a book.

MARIA I know about this.

DAVID Don't you have like somewhere to—My grandfather told me you have a job.

MARIA I do a volunteer at the library. But I take the week free for you.

DAVID I wish you didn't do that. I kind of assumed I would have the days free to work and we'd maybe just run into each other at night.

MARIA Well now we know it is a different situation.

He glances at her briefly, then resumes typing.

MARIA (*cont.*) So. Why you not give your boss the book when he ask?

DAVID He's not my boss. He's my publisher. It's different.

MARIA How is different?

DAVID It's a more equal relationship. If anything, I have the upper hand.

MARIA He pay you?

DAVID Yes, of course.

MARIA You give him the book when you finish?

DAVID Yes.

MARIA Then he your boss.

DAVID Okay. He's not though.

David resumes typing. Maria looks around, picks up an errant dust mite . . .

MARIA So why you not give him the book six week ago?

DAVID I did. I gave it to him. But he thinks it's not funny enough. It's not even supposed to be so funny. It's irrelevant. He's a middleman.

MARIA Is for children?

DAVID The book? Obviously not. It's targeted to college students. Smart kids. Readers.

MARIA Is not children's book?

DAVID No. Why would I write a children's book?

MARIA Your first book was children's book.

DAVID *The Running of the Bulls* was not a children's book! It was a young adult novel.

MARIA It seem more like for children.

DAVID Well, you can read it, I'll get someone to send you a copy, and you'll see—

MARIA I read it already. Two times I read it.

DAVID Did you?

MARIA Of course. My family write a book of course I read.

DAVID The family didn't write the book, *I* wrote the book.

MARIA But I think was for children.

DAVID Well, I wrote it, so I know who I wrote it for. I wrote it for young adults.

MARIA That is what children are, young adults.

DAVID It's a completely different genre. It's not relevant. Anyway, it was an antifascist allegory!

MARIA What this means?

DAVID It means the story's not supposed to be taken literally. It's a metaphor. You probably didn't fully understand the story.

MARIA Story was about talking animals.

DAVID Talking *bulls*! And they were representative of the oppressed populace under General Franco.

MARIA And they each must have a birthday party in the jail.

DAVID The birthday party is a metaphor for stunted growth! And the jail is a metaphor for—for Spanish jail!

MARIA And the animals who not talk too much must wear a silly hat.

DAVID The hat is about mind control, which is why they can't talk! It's a thinly veiled allegory and an allusion to Hemingway and Orwell that literally any eighth grader would understand!

MARIA Is a very strange story but many people buy, I think.

DAVID It sold 64,000 copies worldwide. It was translated into Korean.

MARIA Is good, no?

DAVID Not when it's selling to children. (*as if interviewed:*) You know, it's interesting, it was a great accomplishment, publishing at that age, that kind of early success, it's good, it's not bad, it's good . . . But in retrospect, I'm not really . . . I don't really *like* it that much. You know? I can acknowledge the book's strengths, but I don't *like* it.

MARIA Yes, I think me too.

DAVID Excuse me?

MARIA I read it again just before you come here.

DAVID And you decided you don't like it.

MARIA You want the truth?

DAVID No, not really.

MARIA Okay.

David resumes typing. Long pause—

MARIA (*cont.*) And I think the New York Time no like it either.

DAVID Jesus Christ!

MARIA I read review.

DAVID You read the *Times'* review?

MARIA I put it in frame.

David pushes aside his laptop, marches into the kitchen.

DAVID It was a bad review!

MARIA My flesh and blood in New York Time, I put in frame. Is important newspaper.

Maria pulls the framed review off the wall and holds it proudly.

MARIA (*cont.*) I was thinking you maybe sign it for me.

DAVID What? No. I'm not signing a bad review.

MARIA Maybe you write it small. In the corner.

DAVID Absolutely not.

MARIA Maybe just with pencil.

DAVID No. Maria, I'm not signing that. How did you even get it?

MARIA Your grandfather send me.

DAVID Why would he send a bad review overseas? He doesn't even send me birthday cards.

MARIA I like to read about my family.

DAVID Then I'll send you a good review! We had *Newsweek*, we had the AP!

MARIA You not send me nothing. You not call me never!

DAVID I will when I get back. I'll send you a different review. I'll send you *ten* reviews! Please throw that one out. It's embarrassing to me! Please!

MARIA Is on a wall in Poland! Why is embarrassing?

DAVID It just is. I shouldn't have to explain myself! I will send you a better review if you feel like you really need one—

MARIA (*an explosion*) I don't want better review! I want New York Time review!

Maria aggressively slams a jar of pickles down on the table.

MARIA (*cont.*) You eat pickle. Is no meat.

DAVID (*quieted by her outburst*) Okay, sure. Okay.

MARIA You not eat nothing today.

DAVID Yeah, sorry. I'm not that hungry.

MARIA Because you not eat nothing.

DAVID I tend not to eat when I'm writing. It's inhibiting.

MARIA Your mother will yell at me if she know you eat nothing.

DAVID My mother's not going to yell at you. She doesn't care.

MARIA She's your mother. (*beat*) When I come to your house, she make beautiful fruit salad. Look like art. Cut melon in different shapes. Like a picture.

DAVID Did she?

MARIA You no remember?

DAVID No.

MARIA Your mother, she is a good cook.

DAVID I feel like I don't remember her ever cooking anything.

MARIA No, she cook all the time.

DAVID Yeah, I don't think she did.

MARIA No, she cook always.

DAVID Well I grew up with her, so.

MARIA Your mother is a nice woman.

DAVID She is.

MARIA (*sadly*) And she is beautiful woman.

DAVID Okay.

MARIA Is she still so beautiful?

DAVID My mother? I don't know, she looks the same. That's weird. Don't ask me that.

MARIA I mean, the father is nice too. But the mother? This is something unusual.

DAVID Great.

MARIA You no remember me? I come to your house. 1993. March.

DAVID Yeah, I'm sorry, I don't remember.

MARIA You put on a little play for Jerzy, for me. You and your sister pretend you on a boat. It was not such a good play—

DAVID Well, with limited resources, it's difficult to fully realize a vision—

MARIA And your sister play like a pirate man. She look like a man anyway, so is good for the role. You no remember?

DAVID (*laughing*) I definitely don't remember that, no.

MARIA Well, you were young boy.

DAVID Not that young.

MARIA I think you too young to remember me.

DAVID No, I was probably ten or eleven.

MARIA Yes, is young. Too young to remember an old woman at your house.

DAVID Hmm. Well I think I would have probably—

MARIA You were too young! Is it!

They eat in silence.

MARIA (*cont.*) In 1951 I go to America for eleven months. I stay with your grandfather and his family. In The Queens.

DAVID Just Queens.

MARIA His sister, Ruthie, she want to go out every night. At time she was married to famous artist. She want to take me out, show me to her friends. "Look at my cousin. From Poland. From war."

DAVID That's nice.

MARIA No, is not nice. (*beat*) She bring me to meet Elizabeth Bishop.

DAVID Elizabeth Bishop, the poet?

22

MARIA She tell me before we go to her apartment, "Lizzie is very close friend. Very good friend." She call her name Lizzie but is not her name, you know. She tell me, "Maria, don't talk about the war. Don't make Lizzie sad." Everyone else, she tell me "You talk about war, they want to know what happen to the European Jew." But Lizzie, she tell me, "Keep it light." Keep it light, I no understand. I think she mean, Don't turn off the light at Elizabeth's apartment. I think, I am guest, why would I do such a foolish thing? But when we get to the apartment, first thing Elizabeth say is, "Tell me about war."

DAVID (*laughing*) Of course.

MARIA And I am perplex. I look at Ruthie and I see she is also perplex.

DAVID So what did you do?

MARIA I tell Lizzie, "No. I will not tell you about war." (*beat*) Ruthie not introduce me to any more friends.

DAVID Can I ask you about it?

MARIA About?

DAVID About the war. I'm kind of interested.

MARIA (*affecting nonchalance*) Of course you ask me! I am like open book.

DAVID Are you sure? I don't want to make you uncomfortable.

MARIA Sha, uncomfortable! What you want to know?

The telephone rings.

DAVID Yeah, maybe just don't pick it up this time— (*she does*) Okay!

MARIA *Hello? Yes? I received the letter. No, I'm sorry, I can't. Thank you for calling.* (*hangs up*) It was for fake blind people again.

DAVID That's shocking.

MARIA So what you want to ask me?

DAVID Right, if you don't mind, I would love to know—I'm very curious about your experiences.

MARIA David, stop this, you are nervous. I am me! You ask.

DAVID Okay, sorry. So. My mother told me a little bit about you— about your family—during the war.

Uncomfortable, Maria stands up quickly and enters her room.

MARIA I forget what I need from here. (*sitting down, pretending to laugh at herself:*) I am losing my mind rapidly. You continue.

DAVID Okay. Thank you. So, I know, I know a little bit about your family.

MARIA Me too. What you know?

DAVID I know that you lost—that you lost your whole family.

MARIA Not lost, they all die.

DAVID Right.

MARIA My brother shot in front of my face. Do you like the pickles?

DAVID What, yeah, they're fine.

MARIA Different from American pickles, I think. Maybe not so good.

DAVID No, they're good. I don't mind them.

MARIA You eat anything you want. Zenon take me food shopping tomorrow.

DAVID All right, thank you. So you went to live with your babysitter's family. Is that right?

MARIA Yes, I live there.

DAVID And Jerzy was her son, right?

MARIA Why you ask me questions? You know the whole story.

DAVID No, I don't. I only know a little bit. I'm just sort of interested.

MARIA Is very interesting.

DAVID But I don't want to make you uncomfortable.

MARIA What you talk, uncomfortable? Is no problem.

DAVID All right. How long did you live with them?

MARIA Seven year.

DAVID And they hid you, or . . . ?

Maria nods slightly, choked.

DAVID (*cont.*) And did you know that, like, your family had been—

Overwhelmed, Maria slides her chair back abruptly and moves to the fridge. David quiets, uncomfortable. She stares in the fridge.

MARIA So what is title of your new book?

DAVID Sorry about that, Maria.

MARIA What is name of new book?

DAVID It's an expression, it's an English expression. I don't know if you would know it. Maybe I can ask you another time, I didn't mean to make you upset—

MARIA What is name of your new book?

DAVID It's called *Mindreader.* Cause I thought you might want to start from the beginning—

MARIA What does this mean, The Mindreader?

DAVID I didn't mean to make you uncomfortable or to pry—

MARIA Tell me what this mean, The Mindreader.

Maria busies herself, boiling a pot of water.

DAVID A mindreader is a person who has the ability to—who can hear other people's thoughts. And it's not The Mindreader. It's just *Mindreader*.

MARIA I think The Mindreader is maybe better.

DAVID Okay. But as the writer of it—seeing as it's mine—I kind of like it just as *Mindreader*.

MARIA Good. You no change it just because I tell you.

DAVID I wouldn't do that.

MARIA You must stay in your own mind, trust yourself, David. But maybe also change the title. I think it sound better.

DAVID You're a confusing person.

MARIA You too.

DAVID I know.

MARIA So this thing—*Mindreader*—this is not a real thing.

DAVID Of course it's not real.

MARIA So why you make up something fake?

DAVID It's a science fiction novel. It's supposed to be about something that's not real. But good science fiction—the kind I'm interested in—makes some comment on the real world. It says something about society in a way that other forms of literature—

MARIA I understand, I understand. I think is good idea.

DAVID You do?

MARIA Yes, I think you know this.

DAVID Well it's nice to hear it.

MARIA But you say book is also supposed to be funny.

DAVID Right.

MARIA And you can do this?

DAVID Do what?

MARIA You are funny?

DAVID Yeah. I'm funny.

MARIA (*as though learning new information*) Oh.

DAVID I can be very humorous. You can't tell?

MARIA You seem more angry I think.

Maria takes the kettle and pours two cups of tea.

MARIA (*cont.*) You come shopping tomorrow?

DAVID No, I don't think I can.

MARIA Why? What you do?

DAVID I'm trying to finish a book. I think I may have mentioned it to you several dozen times.

MARIA But you no work. I hear you. You say "I am working on book," but I can hear you.

DAVID What do you mean?

MARIA I know you not pushing on computer. I hear you.

DAVID You can hear that I'm not typing?

MARIA I hear everything.

DAVID That's frightening.

MARIA Is small flat.

DAVID Well, why do you care what I'm doing?

MARIA Because if you in my house and not pushing on computer, you should be with me.

DAVID Okay, well, I promise I'll work tomorrow, I'll *push*, I'll get something done. It's not hard to write something, it's just—

MARIA So why you no do it?

DAVID I could write a book easily. It's a little more difficult to write something good. To write something people like—to write something people buy.

MARIA You want to be famous. Is it?

DAVID No. I would like to be acknowledged, but no, not famous, not necessarily.

MARIA I think this is not a good thing.

DAVID You're entitled.

MARIA I tell you joke—is Polish joke—you understand me more. Little bird sit in a field. A cow walk by and go to bathroom all over little bird. But little bird get up, is not dead, and climb out of cow remains and clean himself with tongue and feathers. Is disgusting maybe to you but is not important. When the bird is clean, he fly away and sit on wire—the most high wire in the village—and he sing a song, is happy. A big bird—hawk, I think— hear him singing, fly down and eat the bird. Now he die for real. So.

DAVID (*beat*) In America, we have jokes that are funny.

MARIA You don't understand it maybe.

DAVID No, it's a nice story. I'll try to find a way to squeeze it into my book.

MARIA Yes, I think you not understand.

DAVID Well, it was a little difficult to follow with your accent. (*beat*) So what does it mean?

MARIA Is better to sit in cow remains than to fly high and sing. You sit in cow bathroom and it smell and is dirty but is safe and you know you will not be eat by hawk bird.

DAVID That's very progressive. Did you learn that from Stalin?

MARIA I learn this from many people.

David, momentarily overcome, moves to her. The telephone rings. David watches her as she grabs it.

MARIA *(cont.)*   *Hello? Yes I received your letter. I did read it. I know. Thank you. Of course. No, thank you for calling. Goodbye. (hangs up)*

DAVID I'm sorry. That they keep calling you.

MARIA I am used to it. I think is maybe more bad for the boy who must call me all day.

DAVID Maria. Maria. Can I tell you something? This guy I know—a friend of mine—this guy I know, he wrote a novel, a best seller, on his cell phone.

MARIA Is good subject to write about.

DAVID No, he didn't write it *about* his cell phone. He wrote it literally on his cell phone. He text-messaged himself one paragraph a day on his subway ride to work. Text messages are like little notes you can send through a cell—

MARIA I know about SMS. What is story?

DAVID It's about a homeless man on the G train—on the subway in New York. It's like a day in the life of this one guy.

MARIA Is good, no?

DAVID It's meandering. It's not—it's fine, it's just stupid though because people are only buying it because he wrote it on the subway. He went on Letterman. It's not the book that people are buying, it's the story of how he wrote it and it just seems like bullshit, kind of.

MARIA You come to Poland.

DAVID So?

MARIA You come to Poland to write the book. He just go on subway.

DAVID Yeah, well I came to Poland because I thought—because I have a relative here.

MARIA I live here.

DAVID Right. And I wanted to visit you.

MARIA No, you want to write your book.

DAVID But I could have gone anywhere. I thought it would be nice to come here though. To come see you. You're my family.

MARIA I think you maybe just come here to write the book.

DAVID Maria, I was trying to share . . . I thought I should tell you about this guy because I wanted to tell you that I feel at all times—like I don't know where—or what I'm going to—I feel like the world is just unfair and I wanted to share that, with you.

MARIA (*beat, gently*) Come, David. We take our tea in the other room. We watch Wolf Blitzer. Is American.

DAVID I know who he is.

Maria leaves David alone. He remains seated, staring into his mug. Maria enters the TV room, places her tea on a small table and flips on CNN International.

WOLF BLITZER History was made in Washington this week when the President warmly welcomed the president of Vietnam to the White House. I spoke with President Triet during his Washington visit. Mr. President, thank you for joining us. Welcome to the United States.

In the kitchen, David grabs the framed NY Times review.

He sits at the table and reads it, genuinely pained. He removes it from the frame and holds the thin paper in his hands. He looks at it in disgust, wanting to rip it apart . . .

Instead, David grabs a pen, quickly signs his name on the article and fits it back into the frame. He opens the cabinet and tries to silently place it back but he rustles the pots and pans loudly.

MARIA David, don't break the house.

DAVID Sorry. I'm coming.

David brings his tea into the TV room. He sits next to Maria, placing his tea next to hers. The lights begin to fade.

WOLF BLITZER Mr. President, did you ever think, during the war, that you would be the president of Vietnam and that you would come to the United States and would be warmly received at the White House? (*translator answering:*) No. I never think this would happen.

BLACKOUT—

The next day, late afternoon

Lights up on the kitchen as the front door rattles open. A bear of a man,
ZENON, *enters carrying several grocery bags.*

Zenon takes a shot glass and a bottle of vodka from the cabinet and pours a
shot. He drinks it swiftly and pounds his chest with a fist. He pours another
shot.

Zenon takes out a large bowl from the cabinet and fills it with warm water.

David sits on his bed, wearing earphones, listening to an iPod and reading a
Lonely Planet guide to Poland.

The small window is open. All of the picture frames in his bedroom are
facedown.

Maria enters the apartment, wearing a long skirt, giddy.

MARIA   David! We are back with the food.

David does not hear her. She speaks to Zenon in Polish:

MARIA   *I'm putting the cold stuff away. We'll take care of the rest later.*

ZENON   *Do whatever you want.*

Maria empties a bag into the refrigerator as Zenon takes out an old razor
and shaving cream from the cabinet and brings a stool to the counter.

Maria struggles up to the counter and sits on it, her legs dangling off. Zenon
sits on the stool, lifts Maria's skirt to just above her knees, rolls her stockings
down and begins shaving her lower legs, using the basin of warm water.

MARIA   *Do it gentle. Try not to cut me.*

ZENON   *Don't tell me what to do.*

MARIA   *They're my legs! Be gentle!*

ZENON   *Okay! Calm down!*

In David's room, he takes a hit of weed off his pipe. He blows the smoke toward the open window. He takes the earphones out and, unbalanced, heads into the kitchen, stopping when he sees them shaving:

DAVID What the fuck!

MARIA Hello, David.

ZENON *Hello, David!*

MARIA He shaving my legs.

David leaps back into his room, as though having witnessed a murder, and takes a huge hit off his pipe.

DAVID Oh my god oh my god oh my god.

MARIA David! Is okay. You come back. He shaving my legs.

ZENON *He hates this?*

MARIA *No! It's fine. Continue.*

DAVID Who is that man and what is he doing to you?

MARIA Is Zenon. I tell you, he shaving my legs.

DAVID Right. Why?

MARIA He used to shave his mother legs and she die one year ago.

DAVID That's not really a sufficient explanation for what I just witnessed.

MARIA He like doing it, it remind him of dead mother. I need my leg should be shave, is good agreement. Now you come in and say hello. You be nice. (*to Zenon:*) *He is a nice boy, but it is difficult to see this.*

David jumps on the sill and attempts to close the small window. It won't budge. He leaves it open and walks back into the kitchen, very stoned.

DAVID Hello, Maria. I'm sorry I reacted that way before, I thought you were being coital.

MARIA Is okay. Zenon, this is David. David, say hello to Zenon.

DAVID Hello, Zenon. Thank you for shaving my second cousin.

ZENON (*speaks rapid Polish to David*) *We just bought you more food than your body will probably tolerate.*

DAVID Really. On behalf of our whole family. We appreciate you coming here weekly, or biweekly, or whatever you do, and shaving this woman's hairy, insulated legs. But, with all due respect, I'm getting a little nauseous watching you two do that. Excuse me.

David walks to the fridge and grabs a juice, drinking out of the carton. Maria says to Zenon:

MARIA *Try not to bother him, he's writing his book.*

ZENON *I don't plan on it.*

MARIA So, David, how is the book?

DAVID What book?

MARIA You almost finish?

DAVID While you were out, it won a Pulitzer.

MARIA What you say?

DAVID I said while you were out shopping for food, it won a Joseph Pulitzer Prize.

MARIA Is okay.

DAVID For literature. For fiction. You know what the Joseph Pulitzer Prize is, Maria?

Maria speaks to Zenon in Polish as David rambles:

MARIA *He's actually a very famous writer in America. Like a little Harry Potter.*

ZENON *He knows Harry Potter?*

DAVID Zenon, you know what the Joseph Pulitzer Prize is? I'm still in shock. About the award. We're all thrilled. We're over the moon! The necessary calls have been made!

Zenon shaves. David stares at his own hand, stoned. Pause.

DAVID Dzien dobry, Zenon!

ZENON Dzien dobry?

DAVID Dzien dobry!

MARIA What is this, David? You learn Polish?

DAVID I learned dzien dobry.

MARIA This mean "Good morning."

DAVID Yeah, I read it means "Hello." A lonely planet told me.

MARIA No, it mean "Good morning."

DAVID Dzien dobry.

ZENON Dzien dobry!

MARIA You sound good, David, but dzien dobry is six hour late. You want you should learn Polish?

DAVID Yes! Teach me Polish, Maria!

MARIA Ooh! Is great idea. You know dzien dobry, yes?

DAVID Yes!

ZENON Dzien dobry!

MARIA This mean "Good morning," David.

DAVID Good morning, Maria!

MARIA But now is evening. You say dobry wieczor.

DAVID *(greatly mispronouncing)* Dobry giecher.

MARIA Is almost. Try again: dobry wieczor.

ZENON Dobry wieczor, David!

DAVID *(badly)* Dobry fiecha.

ZENON *He will never speak this language.*

MARIA David, you speak good. Is hard language.

ZENON (*as if trying to convince him*) DOBRY WIECZOR, DAVID!

MARIA You say it like Zenon.

DAVID (*suddenly embarrassed*) Maybe. I'll think about it. I don't know.

Maria and Zenon speak to each other, mentioning "David"—

ZENON *Is David married?*

MARIA *No.*

ZENON *I didn't think so.*

MARIA *He's waiting to meet the right girl.*

DAVID Hey! Are you guys talking about me?

MARIA He want to know if you married. I tell him no.

ZENON *That's a good thing.*

DAVID What did he say?

MARIA He say is good thing.

DAVID Oh. Thank you very much. I was wondering how he felt about that.

MARIA Zenon get divorce from wife. Three year he in divorce.

ZENON (*to David*) *Women are like devils, but on Earth.*

DAVID What did he say?

MARIA He say woman is like devil, but on earth.

DAVID All women? Or just his wife?

MARIA *All women or just your wife?*

ZENON *All women!*

MARIA All women, he say.

ZENON *But not you, Marysia.*

MARIA But not me, he say.

David ambles offstage, into the bathroom, and we hear him splash water on his face.

Zenon finishes shaving Maria's legs. He places the razor and the bowl in the sink. Maria rolls up her stockings and replaces her skirt over her legs.

MARIA *Thank you. I feel ten years younger.*

ZENON *You look twenty years younger! You're beautiful!*

MARIA David, we are finish shaving, you come back in.

DAVID Are you dressed? Let me know, next time, if you feel compelled to disrobe and—

MARIA Stop talking. Now you meet Zenon nicely. Shake his hand.

DAVID Okay, hello, Zenon.

David reaches out and Zenon devours his hand. He speaks in Polish, gesturing to David's body and laughing.

ZENON *I think you're the skinniest American I've ever seen.*

DAVID What did he say?

MARIA He say you are the most skinny American he ever see.

DAVID Okay, well you could tell him that I don't really feel like being objectified.

MARIA Is okay, David, Zenon is not—he is not cultured man like you and me.

DAVID Tell him that since I learned a little Polish, he should learn some English.

MARIA He will not be good at this.

DAVID Hey, Zenon! You want to learn some English?

Zenon looks to Maria, unsure.

ZENON *What's going on?*

DAVID You! English!

ZENON *What the hell is he telling me?*

MARIA *He wants to teach you English.*

ZENON *Ha, English!*

DAVID Zenon, say "Good morning."

MARIA David, I think this is not a good idea.

DAVID (*enunciating*) Good. Morning.

MARIA *It means "Good morning."*

DAVID Say "Good morning," Zenon!

ZENON Good. Morning.

DAVID That actually sounded pretty good.

MARIA Yes, I am surprise. *You sound good, Zenon!*

ZENON (*celebratory*) *I know!*

DAVID Okay, settle down. Say "Table."

ZENON Table.

DAVID (*lifts his shoe in the air*) Shoe! Say "Shoe"!

ZENON (*mimics David, picks up shoe*) Shoe! (*to Maria*) *I'm so much better learning English than he is learning Polish.*

DAVID What did he say?

MARIA Nothing. I don't know.

ZENON *It's like trying to teach a dog to talk.*

DAVID Tell me what he's saying.

MARIA He say he is better learning English—more better than you learning Polish.

DAVID He said that?

ZENON *He must not have gotten his brain from you because at least you're smart.*

DAVID What was that?

MARIA Uh, is not a compliment.

DAVID Tell me.

MARIA He say that you did not get your brain from me because I am very smart.

DAVID Really?

MARIA Is not very nice.

DAVID No.

Maria looks at David for a moment and turns to Zenon:

MARIA Zenon, say "Shit."

David sputters a laugh, shocked. He looks at Maria, who stares at Zenon, poker-faced.

ZENON Shit. *What does this mean, "shit"?*

MARIA *It means "headache."*

DAVID What did you say?

MARIA I tell him that "shit" mean "headache."

David cracks up as Zenon points to his own head:

ZENON Shit!

Maria and David laugh as David clutches his head:

DAVID I had such a throbbing shit this morning!

ZENON (*laughing with them proudly*) SHIT!

DAVID Why did you do that?

MARIA I don't know.

ZENON SHIT!

MARIA It was not nice to do.

DAVID Yeah, but it's really funny.

MARIA I know.

DAVID Hey Zenon, say "Asshole"!

MARIA Oh god, David!

ZENON ASSHOLE? *What is "asshole"?*

MARIA *It means "a small computer."*

DAVID What did you tell him? What did you say?

MARIA I tell him . . . I tell him "asshole" mean "computer."

Maria laughs as Zenon puts his arm around David:

ZENON *My wife never let me use her "asshole."*

DAVID What did he say?

MARIA He say his wife will not let him use the asshole.

Maria and David crack up as Zenon stands proudly, impressed with himself. He pours another shot.

DAVID That was—you're funny, actually.

MARIA Sha, you are funny.

DAVID No, you are. I may have come up with the "asshole" bit, but the initial gag—the initial gag was yours. That was yours, Maria.

MARIA   Please, it was both maybe.

DAVID   No, I mean it! Good work.

Zenon drinks the shot and pounds his chest. The vodka bottle is now empty.

ZENON   *I love English! Where's the vodka?*

DAVID   What did he say?

MARIA   He say he like English and want to know if we have more vodka.

DAVID   This man is a taxi driver?

MARIA   Yes.

DAVID   People actually pay to sit in the car that this alcoholic caveman operates?

MARIA   Yes, is bad I know. What can I do?

DAVID   Stay off the road.

MARIA   David, you get him the vodka you buy for me. Is in your bag.

DAVID   But that was a gift. I don't want to give it to this guy.

ZENON   *What's up with the vodka?*

MARIA   *Hold on.*

ZENON   *I'm on a schedule!*

MARIA   David, you get him bottle.

DAVID   No.

MARIA   David, he drive me every week.

DAVID   So what? He insulted me.

MARIA   I know.

DAVID And he shaves your legs and that's disgusting. You shouldn't let him do that.

MARIA Maybe. But you go to your room and you get him the bottle.

DAVID (*beat*) No.

MARIA David, you move to Poland and you take me to the food store every week. And you carry my food up to my apartment three staircases and you put away food. And you change my light when it go out and you take me to the post office so I can buy notebook present for my cousin! Or you go to your room and you get the bottle for Zenon!

The telephone rings. Maria answers it:

MARIA *Hello? Yes? I did receive the information. I looked through it . . .*

Zenon becomes impatient. He says to David:

ZENON *I got a pickup. Tell her I said goodbye.*

Maria, still on the telephone, waves Zenon off. Zenon opens the door to leave.

DAVID Hey, Zenon. (*extends a hand:*) Go fuck yourself.

ZENON (*shakes David's hand, laughing*) Dzien dobry! Good morning!

Zenon exits, Maria still on the telephone.

MARIA *No, but thank you for calling. Goodbye.*

Maria hangs up the telephone.

DAVID So, that's too bad. Zenon had to leave.

MARIA He was angry?

DAVID No, he seemed all right. I hope he's drunk enough to drive home.

MARIA You come here for more than one week if you going to make the trouble.

DAVID Sorry, I just don't think you should reward him for basically taking full advantage—

MARIA You not know nothing about me and Zenon.

DAVID So tell me.

MARIA It's not for you to know. I need some things, I need—A woman needs some things—

DAVID Oh! (*rescuing her*) I'm starving, Maria! Did you get me something to eat?

MARIA Yes, I buy you special vegetarianski. The girl in the store show me this. (*removes a block of tofu from the fridge*) She say is just like meat. She has ring going through her nose, I don't know.

DAVID You shouldn't trust everybody. But this is fine, it's tofu, it's very healthy.

MARIA And I get a surprise plate of brownies!

Maria pulls out a huge tray of brownies.

DAVID You think that's going to be enough?

MARIA Is a lot, I know.

DAVID Are you a den mother?

MARIA Because I think if the tofu is disgusting, we eat more brownie.

DAVID Good thinking.

MARIA And you should dress nicely for dinner.

DAVID This is becoming a bit of an event.

MARIA Is important day: Is first time you eat a meal not on plane. Now, did you bring nice clothing? (*re: his hoodie*) Or you stay in the raincoat the whole time you live here?

DAVID This is as nice as it gets. I just figured—I don't know, it's *Poland*—Do people dress nicely here?

MARIA You put on old jacket from Jerzy. Come, we get from your room.

DAVID Okay. (*realizing*) Wait, don't go in there—

MARIA I want you should look nice for dinner.

DAVID Wait—let me just—give me a minute, I have to put something away, it's not perfectly, it's not clean.

David enters his room and jumps on the windowsill. He tries to close the window but it's jammed open.

In the kitchen, Maria hears the commotion, turns on the faucet for sound and walks to David's room, peering in. Unseen by him, she watches as:

David struggles with the window. It won't close. His pipe sits next to him. He takes a hit and exhales out the window. He tugs on the window again but it won't budge.

David moves to his open manuscript and stares at it, reading his work with disgust. He coughs from the weed and Maria ducks her head out of the room.

David puts his head in his hands and breathes heavily. He forcefully throws down the manuscript and, in one furious move, jumps on the windowsill and slams the window closed.

DAVID Maria!

MARIA Yes, David. You want I should come in now?

Maria turns off the faucet and enters his bedroom.

DAVID Am I a terrible person? I think I might have some anger directed inwardly. Am I terrible?

MARIA (*gently*) You would like to talk so much.

She sits on the bed at his feet. He stretches out his legs, resting them on Maria's lap. She stares at his feet, unsure, and then clasps them awkwardly. He rustles them in her hands.

DAVID Am I terrible?

MARIA Is okay.

Maria notices that all of the picture frames are facedown.

MARIA (*cont.*) David, I should ask you a question about the pictures.

DAVID Okay.

MARIA Do you know why they all fall down?

DAVID I haven't noticed.

MARIA I think some frames maybe are old, they fall down sometimes.

DAVID Maybe.

MARIA So is accident? (*no response*) Do you still need them to be this way?

DAVID No, I think I'm done. I just found it a little distracting. I was trying to work and they were, they were all staring at me.

MARIA I understand.

DAVID And I don't know who half of them are, so it didn't seem fair.

MARIA You don't know your family?

DAVID I spotted me in one of the pictures, but no, most of them brought back no memories, good or bad.

MARIA I can tell you who they are, if you like.

DAVID Sure, I'd like to get to know them.

MARIA Can I pick them up now?

DAVID Please.

Maria lifts the first picture frame.

MARIA This is the son of Helen. His name Greg.

DAVID That's great. Who's Helen?

MARIA The cousin of your father, you don't know this?

DAVID Never heard of her.

MARIA Greg live in Texas. His wife is name Sue-Ann—is weird name, I don't know, is from Texas. This is Sue-Ann in picture. She is very beautiful, Greg marry her because of this. She is also doctor and she want they should live in Texas. They have little boy, is name Jack, I no have picture but—

DAVID Okay. Next!

Maria lifts the second picture frame.

MARIA This is Judith, she live in California, in the Hollywood.

DAVID Is she related to Helen?

MARIA Of course is related to Helen! Judith mother is Ester, my cousin of course, and son of Ester is Jacob, my second cousin removed from me one time.

DAVID Right. So how does Helen factor in?

MARIA Helen is married to Jacob!

DAVID Wow! Well done.

MARIA I know all of this, is my family.

Maria lifts the third frame; it is the picture of David.

MARIA This I think you know who is. Is like mirror when you in the room. Is nice.

DAVID I thought that one was going to be Helen. Find me one with Helen! I want to meet Helen!

MARIA We go in order.

DAVID Fine.

Maria lifts the fourth picture.

MARIA This is four brothers. Parents are Mark and Karen.

DAVID Relation to Helen?

MARIA Mark is the cousin of Helen.

DAVID Good, continue.

MARIA Four boys is, in this order, Steven, Saul, and these two are twins, look like each other perfectly, is Daniel and Aaron.

DAVID Our family didn't get too creative with names, did they?

MARIA I think is beautiful names.

DAVID Really? Doesn't it seem like they just thumbed through the Bible a few times? Although I guess you get stuck with four boys, you kind of run out of options.

MARIA My husband have four brothers. With him is five. And one sister.

DAVID Jesus.

MARIA Yes, is big family.

DAVID Did you know all of them?

MARIA Of course I know all of them. I live with them for four years I don't leave house.

DAVID What do you mean?

MARIA I stay inside the same house for four years. I never go outside, not one time. Of course I know them.

DAVID Why did you stay indoors for four years?

MARIA Why?

DAVID Yeah. Why?

MARIA Is stupid question David.

DAVID No it's not.

MARIA Yes, is stupid you should ask me this.

Maria lifts the fifth picture. She takes a moment before speaking, staring at the picture.

MARIA (*cont.*) This is Robert. He in the military. In West Virginia. He fight in the Iraq, for what I don't know. He wear glasses in picture but, in other room, I have picture from school, he no wears them. Maybe he start them in 2002. When children get old, the eyes begin—

DAVID Okay, that's enough. It's too much for one day. If we do any more, I'm not going to remember any of them.

MARIA You want to know how Robert is related to Helen?

DAVID No, that's okay. But thanks for noticing. Now. I want to ask you a question, okay? Out of all these people, I want you to tell me who's visited you. Here, in Poland. Not who you've met, but who's visited you.

MARIA Why you want you should know this?

DAVID I just do. I came here.

MARIA To write a book.

DAVID Well, I'm here. I did it. So who, besides me, has come here, Maria?

MARIA Beside you?

DAVID Besides me.

MARIA Saul, son of Mark.

DAVID Okay. When?

MARIA 1998.

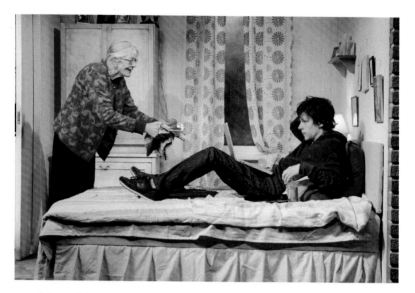

Maria (Vanessa Redgrave) welcomes David (Jesse Eisenberg)
with a roasted chicken (page 11).

Maria and David watch Wolf Blitzer on CNN together (page 30).

Zenon (Dan Oreskes) prepares to shave Maria's legs (page 32).

Maria, David, and Zenon (page 35).

David smokes in his room (page 44).

David and Maria talk early in the morning (page 63).

David packs up, preparing to leave (page 72).

Maria is alone (page 73).

DAVID What month?

MARIA Summer, I don't know. He travel to Berlin and he come to visit me.

DAVID How long did he stay?

MARIA We drink coffee, we have nice time. He tell me about his business—

DAVID How long did he stay here?

MARIA He had meeting in Berlin. He stay with me as long as he could.

DAVID How long.

MARIA He stay maybe three hours.

DAVID Three hours. And he's the only one? You stare at these people every day and only one of them has come here?

MARIA Why you ask me this way?

DAVID Because they're fucking assholes.

MARIA Well. They are all here. In a way.

DAVID Good answer.

MARIA And I meet Saul in 1998. In Poland.

Maria stands over David.

MARIA *(cont.)* You see your grandfather every day?

DAVID Every day? I saw him in August probably. At a wedding.

MARIA He tell me you see him all the time.

DAVID Yeah. I saw him at the wedding.

MARIA If I should live in New York, I would see my family every day. In America, you turn teenager, you move out. In Poland, I think is good, you stay home and live with parents, take care of parents.

DAVID Well, we think of family a little differently in America. You shouldn't make a value judgment. It's not good or bad.

MARIA Is not good or bad. Is bad.

DAVID That's kind of small-minded, you have a limited perspective in some ways, which is understandable. I haven't spoken to my sister in probably six months.

MARIA Your sister is very beautiful.

DAVID What I'm saying is, even though she's my family, I'm not so close with her. I don't think blood is, is necessarily so important.

MARIA You don't think this?

DAVID No, I get along with most of my friends better than her.

MARIA What does this mean, "get along"?

DAVID It means to have a nice relationship.

MARIA So you no think is important? Family like this? Real blood?

DAVID Well, not really, no.

MARIA You know my whole family die, yes?

DAVID I know.

MARIA You know I never have children, yes?

DAVID I know.

MARIA Do you think we get along? (*a moment*) You don't know me, David. Come, we find you the dinner clothing. (*opens the closet*) You choose a jacket, I prepare tofu food, which may be disgusting.

Maria exits into the kitchen and begins preparing the tofu.

David walks to the picture of himself and looks at it. He then lifts the remaining picture frames and finally looks through the clothes, pulling out a sports jacket.

In the kitchen, Maria pulls out and cuts the tofu.

David removes his hoodie for the first time, throws on the jacket and walks into the kitchen.

MARIA *(cont.)*   Ah! I look at you! You are beautiful. Like adult man!

DAVID   Yeah, I feel good, I feel professional! Maybe I'll work a little bit later. Is that okay? After dinner, I think I could get something done. I feel *right,* a little bit. In a suit.

MARIA   You see? You act like a man, you be more quiet when is important, you get the result!

DAVID   Yes, you're talking about discipline!

MARIA   You keep the jacket.

DAVID   Thank you. I think I should start wearing a suit.

MARIA   You dress like a child, you act like a child—

DAVID   I'll buy a tuxedo immediately. From the duty-free shop at JFK—

MARIA   You dress like a man, you act like a man.

DAVID   And I'll walk through New York and everyone will think I just came from a business meeting or something and I'll command some kind of respect! Even on the subway! People will think I'm taking the subway just to *feel* real life! "This guy could be taking a taxi but he's here with us! Good for him!" Good for me.

Maria shuts off the lights and lights a candle.

MARIA   I think if your life was not so good you would maybe finish the book more quickly.

DAVID   You're probably right.

MARIA   Now you do prayer over the tofu. I think is a great idea.

DAVID I don't pray.

MARIA You make it up maybe.

DAVID Maria, I'm not praying over tofu. Why don't you do the prayer?

MARIA I don't know any. You do it. Your grandfather tell me you know every prayer when you were a boy. That you memorize.

DAVID I liked to memorize things.

MARIA He say you are very religious.

DAVID Well, he's wrong. I just liked to memorize. Not just Jewish prayers. I knew every statistic for the New York Knicks. And all the lyrics to "We Didn't Start the Fire." I memorized like a kid memorizes. I knew all of Who's On First.

MARIA What is this?

DAVID Who's on First was a comedic—it was a funny comedy routine.

MARIA Funny like your children's book?

DAVID My young adult novel? Yes, funny like that.

MARIA So you tell me then.

DAVID What?

MARIA Tell me Who's on First. Maybe you do it as a prayer.

DAVID I'm not doing that. I'm not praying Who's On First over a block of tofu. And it's a seven-minute dialogue. I would need some prep time.

MARIA Okay, then we just eat.

DAVID Sounds good.

They begin to eat the tofu. Maria drinks a lot of water.

DAVID *(cont.)* So, you've never had tofu before?

MARIA I have no reason for this.

DAVID Well, I'm honored to witness your first time. What do you think?

MARIA I think is good. I like it very much.

DAVID That's great. I'm glad you like it.

MARIA I say that just to make you happy.

DAVID Thank you. It did, it worked.

Maria reaches across the table and places her hand on his. He pulls away quickly like it was an accident—

DAVID *(cont.)* I got an idea.

David runs into his bedroom and fetches the vodka bottle from his bag.

DAVID *(cont.)* Can I open this?

MARIA You think it will make the tofu taste better?

DAVID It couldn't hurt. Will you have some if I open it?

MARIA I maybe will try a little. I don't drink vodka—I don't drink anything like this—since Jerzy die.

DAVID Then it's a big day for you, Maria! Vodka, tofu. I'm turning you into a real bohemian. I'll give you a henna tattoo later, if you want.

David grabs some juice from the fridge and begins pouring the vodka:

DAVID *(cont.)* Tell me how much you want.

MARIA Is enough. David, you want to learn Polish? You put the juice away.

DAVID Really? Okay . . . okay, sure. I could drink it straight. It doesn't matter, really, for me.

MARIA   And sit down please.

DAVID   Why don't we drink these at the same time and then just eat as much tofu as we can so we don't taste it?

MARIA   Okay.

DAVID   Are you ready?

MARIA   I think so.

DAVID   All right, on three, okay? One two three—

They pound back the shots. Maria begins coughing. It becomes uncontrolled.

DAVID *(cont.)*   Hey! Put your hands over your head or something. Raise them! Put your hands over your head. Breathe! Maria! Breathe!

He grabs her arms and raises them for her. Her coughing subsides. She suddenly grabs him with her raised arms, holding him tightly. He freezes in her grasp.

DAVID *(cont.)*   Maria. Let me get you a glass of water.

MARIA   Sit down. *(releases him)* Are you ready?

DAVID   For what?

MARIA   Do you want me to tell you something?

DAVID   Um, okay?

MARIA   You want to know my story?

DAVID   Oh. Yeah.

MARIA   You want to know the bad thing in my life?

DAVID   Very much.

MARIA   I tell you.

She pours and drinks a shot, downing this one.

MARIA (*cont.*) I hope will not bore you.

DAVID It's okay.

She pours and drinks another shot. And another. She pushes the bottle to David. He does a shot.

MARIA And again.

DAVID (*does another shot, overwhelmed:*) Oh, fuck. Oh fuck!

MARIA How do you feel? (*he can't lift his head*) Okay, is enough. Look up at me. You know I was born in Krasnystaw, is small town in Poland, in east of country, by Ukraine—

DAVID (*reeling from the vodka*) Holy fuck—

MARIA David, look up at me when I speak to you. I say I was born in east of Poland—

DAVID I'm good. I just gotta put my head down, I'm listening though. I'm good.

MARIA Is not good, I want you should look at me.

DAVID It's just I weigh like 135 pounds, it affects me very quickly—

MARIA David, do you want to know this or no?

DAVID Yeah, continue. Please.

MARIA In 1939, I am four year old, we live in Krasnystaw, we have money, we have the respect. The Germans come in, they separate the Jewish people and build a ghetto—is one street at the end of the town. Ghetto is like small city and—

DAVID I know what a ghetto is. I read *Night* in high school. (*she glares at him*) Sorry, that's stupid. Continue.

MARIA I remember that we have to leave the house. They come in, speaking German, picking up my things. And my brother is sick. This is the first memory I think I have in my life. He have a cold, you know, is winter and he is sick, is normal. But as they taking my brother, he sneeze on the man—on the officer. Just one time, he sneeze. Is no problem. But they take him to the middle of the square. My mother is screaming and my father cover her on the mouth, I see him do this to her—and they pull my brother—is ten-year-old little boy—and they shoot him in the face. Because he sneeze in winter.

The telephone rings, shocking them—

DAVID Jesus fucking Christ! Maria, do not pick that up!

MARIA Excuse me, David. *(picking up phone) Hello? Yes? I am fine. No I have time—*

DAVID Maria, hang up the fucking phone—

MARIA David, ssh! *Yes, I received the information, but . . . No, I'm sorry, thank you for calling. And good night to you. (hangs up)* I continue now. After they do this thing, we must walk to the ghetto. Is poor neighborhood, we never go there for any reason, but now is supposed to be the home. I ask my mother why they do this to my brother and she whisper to me that it is my father fault, you know, because he cover her on the mouth—is not a nice thing to say, but . . .

DAVID Holy shit, Maria.

MARIA Yes, don't say that.

DAVID I'm sorry, that's just fucked up.

MARIA We live in this ghetto, is like little flat, I don't remember and one day my nanny come. She is Catholic woman, I stay at her house sometimes when my parents need help before the war. My mother kiss me, say she will see me soon and give me to this woman. The nanny take me—not my older brother because you know he has the penis cut, they know who is Jewish—and my mother pay the nanny to take me. She is smart, she give her everything we have. So I live with this family. The children don't speak to me, is okay, but the nanny don't want me to live in the house, I know this. I am Jewish and someone know about this, they kill the whole family.

(*slows*) So, one day, the nanny come into the basement, where I sleep, and she ask me to say thank you to her. I say thank you. And then she ask me to tell why I must say thank you. You know, what she is doing for me, why I should thank her. I don't know what I should say. So I ask her, "When my parents come back to get me?" And she take me on the wrist like this (*holds David's wrists*), holds them very hard and tell me that they take my parents to Belzec— you know, to breathe in the gas.

(*beat*) And then she ask me again, why I must say thank you to her.

The telephone rings. Maria lunges for the phone but David seizes her arm and they stare at each other.

Suddenly, David stands, grabs the phone and violently slams it down on the receiver. He lifts the phone again and slams it down two times.

David runs into his bedroom and sits on the bed, his head buried in his hands. In the kitchen, Maria, unmoved, takes the tray of brownies and places them on the table.

MARIA (*cont.*)   David, you want you should eat dessert?

DAVID (*wipes his wet face*)   I'll be right in, Maria.

MARIA   David, you come back. You do me something.

DAVID   I'm coming.

MARIA   I want you should do the comedy now.

DAVID   What?

MARIA   You tell me Who's on First.

DAVID   I don't really feel like doing that right now, if you don't mind—

MARIA I do mind. I tell you a story, you tell me one—

DAVID But that's a two-person routine, Maria. I'm just me.

MARIA I understand. Maybe you put on hat, so I know who is what person.

DAVID I don't want to wear a hat.

MARIA So maybe you hold the tray of brownies—When you lift up is one man, when you put down is other man. (*pointedly:*) Please you do it, David.

DAVID I don't know. I feel silly—I—(*she thrusts the tray forward*) Maria, I— I'll lift *one* brownie.

MARIA Is fine. Begin.

DAVID Okay. Are you ready? I feel like an idiot. One second.

David does a shot of vodka. He picks up a brownie and begins, lackluster:

DAVID (*cont.*) Well let's see who we have on the bags, Who's on first, What's on second, I Don't Know is on third This is so silly—

MARIA You continue anyway.

DAVID (*awkwardly sets down the brownie*) That's what I want to find out. (*lifts the brownie*) I say Who's on first, What's on second, I Don't Know's on third. (*takes a bite*)

MARIA If you going to eat brownie, this is not going to work.

DAVID Oh. Sorry, I didn't realize. Then give me a second— (*takes a swig of water to wash it down*) All right. I'm not starting over though, I'll start from "I Don't Know's on third."

MARIA Is fine.

He picks up a new brownie—

DAVID I Don't Know's on third. (*sets it down*) Are you the manager? (*brownie up*) Yes. (*brownie down*) And you don't know the fellows' names. (*up*) Well, I should. (*down*) Well then who's on first? (*up*)

Yes. I mean the fellow's name. Wait, sorry, that was supposed to be down. (*puts brownie down*) I mean the fellow's name. (*picks it up, back on track*) Who. (*down*) The guy on first. (*up*) Who. (*down*) The first baseman. (*up*) Who. (*down*) The guy playing first base. (*up*) Who is on first! (*down*) I'm asking you who's on first. (*up*) That's the man's name! (*down*) That's who's name? (*up*) Yeah! (*down*) Well go ahead and tell me!

MARIA   Okay, I get it. Is enough.

Blackout—

Six hours later

The lights are dim. 3A.M. Maria sits up in her bed with a Sudoku book and a night-light. David sleeps in his bed.

Suddenly, David falls out of bed onto the floor. He shoots up, panicked, grabs his pipe and baggie of weed. He jumps up onto the windowsill but slips off, grabbing his foot.

DAVID Ah! Fuck me!

MARIA David?

DAVID Yeah. Yeah. (*runs into her room, heart racing*) Hey, what's up? Are you up? I just got up.

MARIA What happen to you? You wet.

DAVID Is it cold in here? It feels cold. I think I just, I think I had a nightmare or something.

MARIA Then is good time for the company.

DAVID Sure, yeah. Maybe I'll just—I think I'll maybe just sit down for a minute. (*flops down on the floor at the edge of her couch*) Wow!

MARIA You maybe tell me what nightmare was about.

DAVID Yeah? Is that a good idea? It's good to exorcise. That's good advice. Sure. I'll tell you.

MARIA Okay. Begin.

DAVID Right. So I was in this kind of corporate office. Everything was so real. And I don't go in these, so I don't know how I know. Anyway, I was waiting for an elevator—

MARIA Wait, you wait here. (*she fetches a wet washcloth from the kitchen*) Keep speaking to me.

DAVID Okay, so I don't know what I was doing there but I was waiting for an elevator. And, when it came, I stepped in and there was one other guy inside. He was just like a businessman, he was clean-cut, anonymous. And the doors closed and I criticized him in my mind. And we started going down and the elevator starts picking up speed. I didn't hear anything snap—a cable or anything—but I know what's happening, the guy knows what's happening and we're falling. (*she presses the washcloth to his neck*) Thank you. And then the guy looks at me and I see his eyes and he's suddenly, like, *real* to me and then we both just looked at each other, knowing we would be the last thing we would both see. And I felt the rush. And I felt it. And I think I fell out of the bed. What do you think it could mean?

MARIA   I think it mean you still drunk.

DAVID   That's true, that's probably it. I guess it's a cliché, a falling-elevator dream. I think I have an unimaginative subconscious, Maria. But it was real. Because it felt real. No. It felt good to tell you though, thank you. It feels good to tell you things.

MARIA   It feels good.

DAVID   I should probably just go back to sleep.

He rests his head against her couch. Pause.

MARIA   Did you like my story before?

DAVID   It was depressing, really, I guess mostly.

MARIA   There is a different part of it. Maybe will be more interesting to you. Can I say it?

DAVID   Okay?

MARIA   I tell you. When the war finish, people come back to Krasnystaw, you know, people who survive, very few. And a girl—my age—she come back and she see me in the town. I know her from before the war, we play together, and she say hello to me and I pretend to not know her, I am Catholic now, they tell me not to speak to no one. But I need to know what happen in the camp. So I visit with this girl, in secret. She is very sick, she has the tuberculosis disease, but I don't think about this too much. And she tell me about her family, also killed in the camp. But she say she think she has *more* family. In New York, in America.

DAVID What do you mean, more family—?

MARIA Cousins. The people in New York don't know she is born and she die of tuberculosis. Ten-year-old little girl, David, she die before anyone know she is even born. World is not fair, you say. For six year, I think about this girl every day. I remember every part of her story and I start to think this girl is my sister, my family. Her family is my family. And I think to have a family in New York. I picture everybody. New little babies I can hold on to. Old people I can watch die with peace. Say "Remember when he did this or that and I get mad."

DAVID Maria . . .

MARIA So, in 1951, I get marry to Jerzy and I have papers now, no one know who I am before the war and I make a telephone call to organization in Israel. "I think I might have family in New York," I tell them, "this is the name." (*beat*) And now you my cousin.

DAVID (*overwhelmed*) What?

MARIA This is how you are my cousin.

DAVID Why are you telling me this?

MARIA You come to Poland.

He says nothing. She looks at him expectantly.

MARIA (*cont.*) David?

DAVID I was supposed to go Kathmandu. I knew a guy who went there in the eighties and he wrote four novels in two months. I read one of them, it was terrible, but he finished it. But I always thought if I do something, something stupid or dirty or dangerous or life-threatening, I would become creative. That the only thing standing in the way was comfort. But I'm in Szczecin Poland with you Maria and I can't write a fucking word. It's not relevant. (*faces her*) I got rejected from three writers colonies in upstate New York and I applied to one in Scotland but I couldn't afford the room. I knew a guy from college who moved to Nairobi and I was gonna go visit him—maybe cross into Tanzania and go on safari—I don't know what I was thinking, I can't think of anything worse than going on a safari—but he never e-mailed me back. (*gently*) You were a last resort, Maria, I'm sorry. Anyway, there's violence in Kathmandu, there's an insurgency of Maoists—so.

She massages his head. He clasps her hands.

MARIA David, I think you should stay here and live with me.

DAVID Well.

MARIA Is good for you, I think.

DAVID Maybe.

MARIA You can write your books in the other room.

DAVID Maybe.

MARIA I feed you all the meals. I learn vegetarianski recipe.

DAVID That's okay.

MARIA Is good, we don't have so many elevators in Szczecin.

DAVID That's true.

MARIA David? I wonder what you think of what I tell you before.

DAVID Yeah.

MARIA (*becoming desperate*) I don't know what you think about this, David.

DAVID Right. Well, I guess . . .

MARIA Yes?

DAVID I don't know. I don't care.

MARIA Okay?

David abruptly gets up.

DAVID I think I should I call my mother.

MARIA David?

DAVID She worries about me.

MARIA She's not worried.

DAVID It's been a few days.

MARIA She's sleeping now maybe.

DAVID (*beat, softly*) Okay.

MARIA Yes, I think she's sleeping now.

DAVID I'm kind of tired, Maria.

MARIA Is late.

DAVID It is late.

MARIA (*desperately*) David?

He turns around at his doorway.

MARIA (*cont.*) So this—it will be okay? It will be good?

DAVID I'll see you in a little bit.

MARIA I see you tomorrow. It will be Sunday.

David closes the door to his bedroom. Maria stares after him, growing mortified.

Blackout—

SCENE 5

The next morning

Zenon sits center stage at the kitchen table, eating nuts from a bowl by the handful. David's return plane ticket is no longer on the refrigerator door.

Maria is getting dressed in her room. David is sleeping in his room, still wearing the suit jacket.

ZENON *Maria, I'm starving—*

MARIA Shh!

ZENON *I would like eggs.*

MARIA *Zenon! Shh! He's sleeping.*

ZENON *All right, all right. Little punk.*

Maria enters the kitchen.

ZENON (*cont.*) *Let's go already! Wake the kid up.*

MARIA *Maybe we should wait five minutes.*

Zenon grabs an orange from the counter, peels it and eats the whole thing.

ZENON *Did you want some?*

MARIA *No. Thank you.*

Zenon stares at his watch and slams the table with a fist:

ZENON *Come on already! I get pissed off when I wait.*

MARIA *You're a taxi driver.*

ZENON *Exactly!*

David stirs awake. He slides out of bed, very hung-over.

DAVID Hello? I feel like shit. Maria? (*no response*) Maria, are you up?

Maria doesn't move. Zenon jabs her—

MARIA I am awake.

DAVID I gotta puke. Next time, we use a mixer, okay?

David crosses offstage into the bathroom. We hear a steady stream of piss:

DAVID (*OS*) (*sings Neil Young*) "Old man lying by the side of the road with the lorries rolling by, Maria, blue moon sinking from the weight of the load and the buildings scrape the sky . . . "

Zenon walks into David's bedroom and opens David's suitcase. Maria follows Zenon in but hesitates:

MARIA *Zenon, I feel sick.*

ZENON *You gonna help me or not?*

Zenon begins packing David's belongings, which have been strewn about his room. He looks under the bed, pulls socks out, tosses them into the suitcase. He picks up the empty Hellmann's jar, confused, and tosses it in.

Maria eventually joins in, helping Zenon. They pack all of David's stuff, cramming it into the suitcase as David continues singing in the bathroom, unaware:

DAVID (*OS*) (*pissing, singing*) "Cold wind ripping down the alley at dawn and the morning paper flies, Maria. Dead man lying by the side of the road with the daylight in his eyes. Don't let it bring you down, Maria, it's only castles burning, find someone who's turning"—Oh shit— (*we hear David puke*) Holy hell! "And you will come around" (*pukes again*) Whoo! It feels so good to puke, oh it feels so good! Maria, do you ever get to puke?

"You will come around!" (*pukes*) Wow! The relief that follows a good purge, Maria, it's almost worth it. This is really disgusting though. (*We hear the toilet flush and the sink turn on; he is washing his face*) "Don't let it bring you down, Maria, it's only castles burning, Just find someone who's turning" (*he enters from the bathroom*) "And you will come around." I would not go into that bathroom for a few days, if I were you.

David stops, seeing Zenon. Maria eyes the floor.

DAVID (*cont.*)   What's he doing here?

ZENON   *Can we go now?*

MARIA   *Zenon, please.*

DAVID   Maria, should we teach him some new words? Hey, Zenon, say "fuck." Say "fuck!"

ZENON   *What the hell is he saying? I don't have all day.*

MARIA   *Zenon, I feel terrible.*

ZENON   *You have a weak stomach.*

DAVID   Hello! I'm right here! What are you talking about? What's going on?

Maria stares at the floor.

DAVID (*cont.*)   Maria, what the hell's going on? (*sees his suitcase*) Is that my suitcase? Did you pack my suitcase?

MARIA   Zenon take you to the airport now.

DAVID   Is he always three days early for pickups?

MARIA   You have plane in three hours, I think is good you leave now.

DAVID   What are you talking about? My flight leaves on Wednesday.

MARIA   I call and change the ticket. Is free, don't worry.

DAVID   Why would you do that? Why would you change the ticket?

MARIA   Zenon say the security is more time, is good you leave now.

DAVID   Are you kicking me out? What the fuck is this, preschool? Should I go stand in the corner? Maria! Look at me!

David tries to get to his suitcase but Zenon blocks his way.

ZENON   *Where do you think you're going?*

DAVID Get the fuck out of my way. (*pushes Zenon, who pushes back hard*) Maria! Zenon pushed me! He pushed me!

David becomes frantic. He grabs the suitcase from Zenon and begins to unpack it, putting the clothes back into the dresser and his books back on the bed. Zenon picks up everything David puts away, putting it back into the suitcase. They look like children.

ZENON *Hey! Get back here!*

DAVID Who the fuck do you think you are? Maria, why are you doing this!

ZENON *You're a spoiled rich American son of a bitch.*

DAVID (*grabs a sweatshirt from Zenon*) Let fucking go of that! That's mine.

David tugs on the shirt but Zenon easily grabs it and shoves David violently into the wall, making a loud thud. Maria enters David's room.

ZENON *He pushed me first!*

MARIA *Zenon! You wait in the car.*

ZENON *It was self-defense, Maria! He's a fucking American!*

MARIA *Go wait in the car, Zenon!*

ZENON *I'm trying to help you, you ungrateful bitch!*

Zenon storms out of the house, slamming the door. After a moment, he pops back in, politely:

ZENON *I'll be waiting in the car.* (*slams the door again*)

David remains slumped, in pain.

MARIA Did he hurt you, David? (*no response*) Should I get you the ice? (*no response*) David?

DAVID Why are you doing this?

MARIA David, please you should go now.

DAVID Why?

MARIA David, please don't ask me anything.

DAVID Do you care about what you told me last night? Because I don't care—

MARIA I say David, you don't ask me anything!

DAVID Maria, really, it's totally irrelevant. Are you embarrassed? Because I won't tell anybody what you told me—I promise you—

MARIA (*plugs her ears and yells*) David, you stop talking about this right now!

DAVID (*yells even louder in her face*) Maria, I fucking don't care about anything!!

MARIA I think is best you leave now! You come!

Maria grabs David's arms to drag him out but he pulls away and jumps on the bed.

DAVID It's not up to you.

MARIA Is *only* up to me.

DAVID I thought we were getting along. I thought you liked me!

MARIA You are a very hard person to like, David.

DAVID Fuck you.

MARIA You make a problem for me at every minute.

DAVID Like what?

MARIA Like what? We start at the beginning, you come to me three hour late—

DAVID My fucking plane was delayed!

MARIA And I want I should feed you, I want you should eat, I think you are hungry after long plane ride and you tell me you want you should go to sleep—

DAVID So fucking what, Maria! I was tired!

MARIA And you open my window! Ah! Do you open my window! You think I no know about this, but! You tell me you want—you need air! But I see you smoking cigarette outside the window.

DAVID I didn't want to blow smoke inside your house!

MARIA Then you go outside!

DAVID I can't go outside with that! It's not—I don't smoke cigarettes! I have a bit of an issue, I need—yes, I have an issue, but it's mine.

MARIA And when you open my window, and I tell you this, my bill go up. You think I am rich, I buy you food, you think I am just rich!

DAVID Okay! I'm sorry. You're right, I shouldn't have opened the window. (*reaches into his wallet, pulls out some money*) Here! Take this. Please take it.

Maria takes the money and stuffs it into her pocket.

DAVID (*cont.*) Anything else?

MARIA The worst thing!

DAVID Oh yeah? What's that? I left the toilet seat up?

MARIA You hurt the pictures.

DAVID What does that mean? I don't know what that means.

MARIA You turn down all the pictures in my house! Of *my* family!

DAVID I turned down a few pictures! And you didn't care about that. Because you're fucking sane. You didn't care about that!

MARIA Is not your decision!

DAVID Who fucking cares? I turned down some pictures. In my room!

MARIA Is *my* room! You just sleep in it!

DAVID Well, whatever, I put a few pictures down, who gives a shit?

MARIA Who say you could do this? This is my family! This is my life! My relationships I have!

DAVID Maria, I know you don't care about the pictures! I know why you're kicking me out and I'm telling you I don't care about what you told me last night!—

MARIA (*continuing on about the pictures*) They are my people! You don't even know the names! How dare you! You are so stupid, you don't even know the names! They are my family. I know about them. You don't know anything! They are to *me*!

She frantically tries to zipper his suitcase but it's too full and she can't bring the zipper fully around.

MARIA (*cont.*) You are a selfish boy! You are stupid! You don't even know their names! They are not to you! They are to me!

DAVID I know they are.

MARIA So you ask me why you must leave now? Now you know. Because of this! Because of *rudeness*! (*trying to zipper the suitcase*)

DAVID I'm sorry, Maria.

David grabs the suitcase and begins to help her close it. As they do it together, she struggles to push down the top:

MARIA (*pushing*) You are terrible. (*pushes*) You are very terrible. (*pushes*) And you are terrible.

DAVID No I'm not! (*takes her hands forcefully*)

MARIA You are a terrible guest. You are a terrible guest to me, David. You are the guest, David. I hate you!

DAVID Hey! No you don't!

MARIA I do! I do! You are a terrible person, David.

He grabs her tightly. She acquiesces, falling into him.

DAVID I'm not, Maria.

MARIA I hate you.

She weeps, her head buried in his chest. He strokes her.

DAVID I'm not, Maria.

The front door opens, Zenon stands there. Maria and David look up.

ZENON *What's taking so long? Traffic is terrible right now.*

MARIA *(wipes her face)* He's coming.

DAVID What did he say?

ZENON *If we left five minutes ago we would have saved an hour. The way traffic works right now is every five minutes is equal to one hour. I've explained this to you before! You know this, Marysia!*

DAVID Maria. What did he say?

Zenon exits the apartment, closing the door. Pause.

DAVID *(cont.)* What did he say to you?

MARIA He say there is a lot of traffic to the airport.

David nods, grabs his suitcase, fixes his suit jacket and exits the apartment.

Maria stands alone. Pause. She walks into the kitchen. She walks back into his bedroom. She begins to make his bed and finds his hoodie, which was lodged between the bed and the wall. She zippers it up and lays it neatly on the bed. She walks into the kitchen. Pause.

She walks into the TV room and switches on the television. She sits on the couch. She flips through channels, landing on CNN International.

CNN To say that Vietnam's economy is booming is an understatement in the extreme. Last year, exports to the U.S. alone surged by 6.6 billion dollars. Hard evidence that the capitalist reform is sweeping through the communist state.

The telephone rings; it is Sunday. Maria remains seated.

CNN And Intel, the world's largest computer chip maker, is significantly ramping up its presence in this country of 82 million people, investing up to a billion dollars in its operations there. This is a very important turning point for Vietnam, an opportunity to push for more reform to improve the business environment.

The telephone rings again. She turns up the volume on the television. The lights slowly begin to fade—the telephone ringing, drowned out by the television.

CNN Joining the WTO will make the country more dynamic and lessen the time for Vietnam to become a more prosperous nation. And with Vietnam bagging its place as the WTO's 150th member, the door is now open for it to enter an entirely new economic era.

BLACKOUT—

APPENDIX OF POLISH DIALOGUE

Below are Polish translations of the text that appears in italics on the noted page.

SCENE 1

Page 11, line 1: *Halo? Dobrze, a pan? Wszystko dobrze. Tak?*
Page 11, line 5: *Tak otrzymałam. Ale teraz nie mogę. Dziękuję za telefon. Do widzenia.*
Page 12, line 9: *Halo? Tak? Dobrze. Dziekuję. A Ty? Nie, przepraszam. Do widzenia.*

SCENE 2

Page 15, line 6: *Halo? Tak, mam czas. Wiem. Nie, dziękuje. Ale dziękuje za telefon. Nawzajem.*
Page 23, line 27: *Halo? Tak? Otrzymalam list. Nie, przepraszam, nie mogeę. Dziękuję za telefon.*
Page 29, line 8: *Halo? Tak, otrzymałam list. Tak, przeczytalam. Wiem. Oczywiście. Nie dziękuję za telfon. Do widzenia.*

SCENE 3

Page 32, line 15: *Zimne rzczy schowam do lodówki, reszte zostaw.*
Page 32, line 16: *Rób co chcesz.*
Page 32, line 22: *Delikatnie. Nie pokalecz mnie.*
Page 32, line 23: *Nie mów mi co mam robić.*
Page 32, line 24: *To są moje nogi. Delikatnie!*

Page 32, line 25: *Dobra. Uspokój się.*

Page 33, line 12: *On tego nie znosi?*

Page 33, line 13: *Nie! Dawaj . . .*

Page 33, line 22: *Nie widac, ale miły chłopak.*

Page 34, line 3: *Dla Ciebie więcej żarcia niż twoje ciało bedzie mogło tolerować.*

Page 34, line 11: *Ni przeszkadzaj mu. On pisze nowele.*

Page 34, line 12: *Nie mam takiego zamiaru.*

Page 34, line 24: *On jest bardzo sławnym pisrzem w Ameryce. Jak mały Harry Potterek.*

Page 34, line 27: *On zna Harrego Pottera?*

Page 36, line 1: *On nigdy nie będzie mówił w tym języku.*

Page 36, line 8: *David żonaty?*

Page 36, line 9: *Nie.*

Page 36, line 10: *Tak myslałem.*

Page 36, line 11: *Czeka na odpowiednią dziewczynę.*

Page 36, line 14: *To dobrze.*

Page 36, line 20: *Kobiety sa jak diabły, ale na ziemi.*

Page 36, line 24: *Wszystkie kobiety, czy tylko Twoja żona?*

Page 36, line 25: *Wszystkie kobiety!*

Page 37, line 2: *Ale nie Ty, Marysiu.*

Page 37, line 8: *Dziękuję. Czuję się o dziesięć lat młodsza.*

Page 37, line 9: *Wyglądasz jak nastolatka. Jesteś piękna!*

Page 37, line 17: *Jesteś najchudszym Amerykaninem jakiego kiedykolwiek widziałem.*

Page 38, line 3: *Co sie dzieje?*

Page 38, line 5: *Co on mówi? Do cholery?*

Page 38, line 6: *On chce Cię uczyć angielskiego.*

Page 38, line 7: *Ha, angielski!*

Page 38, line 11: *To znaczy dzień dobry.*

Page 38, line 15: *Dobrze, Zenon.*

Page 38, line 16: *Wiem.*

Page 38, line 20: *O wiele lepiej idzie mi angielski niz jemu polski.*

Page 38, line 24: *To jak uczenie psa mowy.*

Page 39, line 5: *Rozumu po Tobie nie ma, bo Ty to chociaż jesteś mądra.*

Page 39, line 19: *Co to znaczy?*

Page 39, line 20: *Ból glowy.*

Page 40, line 11: *Co znaczy?*

Page 40, line 12: *To znaczy mały computer.*

Page 40, line 16: *Moja zona nigdy nie da mi swojej asshole.*

Page 41, line 4: *Kocham angielski. Gdzie jest wódka?*

Page 41, line 17: *Gdzie ta wódka?*

Page 41, line 18: *Poczekaj.*

Page 41, line 19: *Nie mam czasu.*

Page 42, line 13: *Hal? Tak? Otrzymalam informacje. Przejrzałam.*

Page 42, line 15: *Ktos dzwonil po taryfe. Powiedz jemu dowidzenia od mnie.*

Page 42, line 22: *Nie, ale dziękuję za telefon. Do widzenia.*

Page 56, line 10: *Hal? Tak? W porzadku. Mam czas.*

Page 56, line 13: *Tak, otrzymałam informację . . . Nie, przepraszam, dziękuję za telefon, I dobranoc.*

SCENE 5

Page 65, line 7: *Z głodu, umieram, Maria.*

Page 65, line 9: *Chciałbym jajka.*

Page 65, line 10: *Zenon! Cicho! On śpi.*

Page 65, line 11: *Dobra. Dobra. Gnojek.*

Page 65, line 13: *Dobrze idziemy. Budz malucha.*

Page 65, line 14: *Czekaj pięć minut.*

Page 65, line 16: *Chcesz troche?*

Page 65, line 17: *Nie, dziękuję.*

Page 65, line 19: *Chodz. Już. Wkurwia mnie czekanie.*

Page 65, line 20: *Jesteś taksówkarzem.*

Page 65, line 21: *Dokładnie.*

Page 66, line 9:   *Zenon, nie dobrze mi.*

Page 66, line 10:   *Pomożesz mi czy nie?*

Page 67, line 2:   *Idziemy już?*

Page 67, line 3:   *Zenon, proszę.*

Page 67, line 6:   *Co on gada do cholery jasnej? Nie mam czasu.*

Page 67, line 7:   *Zenon, czuję sie strasznie.*

Page 67, line 8:   *Jesteś cienka.*

Page 67, line 25:   *A Ty gdzie idziesz?*

Page 68, line 7:   *He, Wracaj! Wracaj!*

Page 68, line 10:   *Jesteś rozpieszczonym, bogatym, amerykańskim skurwysynem.*

Page 68, line 15:   *On mnie pierwszy popchnął.*

Page 68, line 16:   *Zenon! Czekaj w samochodzie.*

Page 68, line 17:   *To była samoobrona, Mario. On jest pieprzonym Amerykaninem!*

Page 68, line 18:   *Zenon! Czekaj w samochodzie!*

Page 68, line 19:   *Próbuje ci pomóc, ty niewdzięczna suko!*

Page 68, line 22:   *Poczekam w samochodzie.*

Page 72, line 7:   *Dlaczego to tyle trwa? Teraz jest okropny ruch.*

Page 72, line 8:   *On idzie.*

Page 72, line 10:   *Jakbyśmy wyszli pięć minut wcześniej byśmy oszczędzili godzine. Teraz każde pięćminut to stracona godzina. Juz ci to wyjaśniałem! Wiesz o tym Marysiu.*